Over My Dead Body:
The Art of Saying
NO

A Step by Step Journey Towards
Boundaries That Stick

Jen Gaudet

Table of Contents

Acknowledgements

For those of you who know me, have heard me speak, have coached with me, you know I stand firmly by my belief that #togetherwearestronger. This book is no exception.

If I had to do this alone, I can assure you it will never have been written. The reason it exists is because of the constant encouragement of my friends, family, colleagues, mentors, clients, along with the power of the work done in this book. It HAD to be written. Thank you to Kidd Marketing for guiding me through this entire process, holding me accountable to deadlines (definitely not my strong point!) and truly making this book a reality.

I would like to thank my husband, David, who has stood steadfastly by my side as I battled my way towards healthy boundaries, never giving up on me or on our relationship. Thank you for being my rock, and loving me through these amazing transformations.

I would like to thank my mentors and coaches at Health Coach Institute, for opening my eyes to what could be, challenging me to continue to dream bigger, supporting me and stretching me to share my gifts with the world. Without the inspiration and mentorship of these amazing people, I may never have found my way towards setting boundaries, coaching, or this book. Thank you Stacey Morgenstern, Carey Peters, Bill Baren, and Eric Neuner for your amazing leadership and the amazing community you have created with Health Coach Institute. Thank you to my many coaches along the way, and my fellow coaches and colleagues in the HCI community who have played such a large role supporting me. The work that you do in our world is inspiring, and together we are being the change we want to see in the world.

A special thank you to all of my friends and family who have weathered the ups and downs as I reclaimed my own life and transitioned away from traditional healthcare in order to share my learnings with so many more. I had no idea the impact of this work and the places it would take me. Thank you for loving me through the process.

Thank you to each and every one of my clients. Each of you inspires me daily. I feel honored and privileged to have been a part of YOUR journey. I enjoy following your respective successes as they truly motivate me daily.

My final thank you is for YOU, reading this book, deciding to make a change, courageously moving forward towards a life with boundaries. As you fill your cup to overflowing through practicing healthy boundaries which allow for self-care and growth, the ripple effect on those around you will begin to shift our communities and our world for the better. Showing up fully, re-energized and recharged in your day will not only restore your Joie de Vivre, but it will also impact everyone who comes into contact with you. Joy is contagious, and our world needs your full brilliance!!!

"The secret to change is to focus all of

your energy, not on fighting the old, but

on building the new"

~   Socrates

Introduction

When you think about boundaries, what comes to mind? A place beyond which you don't go? A line drawn? If you can, imagine a line drawn in the sand. That line keeps everything you want inside with you, and everything you don't want on the other side of that line. Another practical image is a fence on your property. The fence goes along your property line, it keeps what you want in, and what you don't want out.

Boundaries can be set and held for any area of your life. They can be set for how you're spending your resources and for how you allow people to treat you and speak to you. Boundaries are useful for anything in our physical space or regarding our time, and even for our resources and emotional space. These 'lines in the sand' or 'fences' keep us safe, they keep us respected and protected, and they also provide a sense of privacy when it's needed. Having boundaries is essential in our lives, but knowing how to set them isn't always the easiest.

In which areas of your life could healthy boundaries benefit you? Family, career, spiritual, relationships, self, health, community service? You will find that the stories of people with whom I've worked in this book have set boundaries which have positively impacted MULTIPLE areas of their lives. In this book, you will also find actions you can take today to start YOUR boundaries journey. Let's see what healthy boundaries look like to get started.

Life With Healthy Boundaries

Let's think about life with healthy boundaries. It may look like having a career which excites you. You may wake before your alarm regularly because you've gotten enough quality sleep. You have slept soundly through the night: no waking up at 2 am filled with anxiety or a sense of dread or impending doom worrying over deadlines or "what ifs." No checking your phone in the middle of the night to answer emails or check your calendar and ensure you've got all your tasks lined up for the next day. You were able to fall asleep easily last night; you were completely relaxed, your mind was at ease, and your heart was full.

Your morning routine is relaxing. You set your intentions for your day, clean up, and get ready. Perhaps, you enjoy a hearty breakfast or a cup of coffee. You may get a bit of movement in before leaving for your workday.

You glide through your workday with enough energy left over for your family/ friends/ hobbies at the end of the day. When coworkers or managers knock on your door, you feel comfortable saying that you do not have space on your schedule to be 100% present for an additional task. When you need a solid lunch break of solitude to recharge, you feel comfortable politely declining that lunch invite. In fact, you are able to actually TAKE your lunch break without feeling guilty about all those calls and emails you need to return. You are fully present to your needs, and as a result, you are much more effective and efficient in the second half of your day.

Being able to say NO from a place of love looks like declining that invite to sit at a smoky bar and listen to music that grates on your nerves with your BFF, suggesting instead to have a walking conversation and a quiet dinner...quality time that meets both of your needs without placing you in discomfort.

Perhaps it looks like declining that huge party in favor of an intimate coffee or quality time activity with a loved one on a birthday.

Living a life of healthy boundaries is surprisingly free of resentment, anger, and guilt. You actually WANT to be where you are and CAN be fully PRESENT throughout your days, weeks, and life. As a result, you are excited about plans (rather than dreading them or wondering why you agreed in the first place). You look forward to your day, to your plans (or lack of plans).

Healthy boundaries mean you do not give others permission to have power over you. When someone speaks to you in a disrespectful manner, you speak up and establish the manner in which you prefer to be spoken.

Learning to say NO looks like healthy relationships with yourself and others, real connections to your spouse, children, family, friends. It looks like freedom to choose how to spend your valuable time. Learning to set boundaries allows you to be FREE. Free to choose how to spend your time, love, and money. Free to choose how to learn, how to grow, how to have fun.

Life with good boundaries is amazing! For me, I get to actually have the marriage that I had always wished for. With both myself and my husband setting boundaries, it's freaking awesome because we have quality time. We're busier than we've ever been in our respective careers and lives, and yet we have traveled together (our favorite hobby) way more even than we did before life without boundaries. The difference is now we are really clear on when we're at work it's work, and when we come home, we don't bring work home with us. We are crystal clear that one night out of every weekend belongs to us. We have a date night we hold as a sacred appointment each week. If we're both in town, we have a date night in the middle of the week. Date nights have become non-negotiable. We set and honor Non-negotiable appointments for quality time with each other.

In my workday, one non-negotiable is my yoga or movement session. After a couple sessions with clients, I have a break in which I do yoga, go swimming, take a quick break to move a little, or do something to help keep my energy aligned. I teach my clients how to manage their energy by setting boundaries, even in a super busy workday or clinical practice through 1-2 minute mini-breaks. I practice what I preach: it becomes a non-negotiable appointment in my calendar to have quality time, to take care of my body, to eat lunch.

Once upon a time (just a couple years ago), I didn't take lunch breaks to truly enjoy my food and create that space by choosing working lunches instead. I believed that somehow my patients would suffer or if I just caught up on paperwork and email follow-ups over lunch, I would be more present in the clinic. Now, I schedule my lunch breaks because I prioritize my health, My spouse, my family, my health, travel and serving others are my top priorities which means taking care of myself is honoring these priorities through non-negotiable appointments.

What else has setting, and honoring, healthy boundaries done for me?

We just bought a house as an investment property that we're renting to my daughter, who is about to be 23. Rents here are astronomical, but housing prices are good.

We wanted a healthier boundary with our daughter, which did not include sharing a space. Because rents are so high, she was having difficulty sustaining independent living, returning to our home between leases due to difficulty with finances transitioning to adult life.

We decided together that we would use resources to do that. It's an investment that ultimately our daughter can rent to own. It meets everybody's needs. I am serving my family and making sure she's set for a successful launch. My husband and I talked about it; we came together on it. We have learned what are we willing to do and what are we not willing to do.

Boundaries have saved my marriage and have helped me have a better relationship with my family. We determine what is non-negotiable. We set boundaries and honor them. My husband and I are busier now than we have ever been while being closer now than we have ever been.

I have created boundaries in career, relationships, family, friends, self-care, giving back, my business, and my health. As a result, I have the same amount of time (24 hours in a day) yet am able to honor all areas of my life with the balance I desire.

For me, healthy boundaries mean I am finally free of guilt and resentment around doing things I don't feel inspired to do. I have much fewer "obligations" which receive any thought or time in my life. I no longer worry about what everyone else will think if I choose not to subject myself to a group event out of alignment with my values.

Destruction From Unhealthy Boundaries

So why am I so passionate about this? Because being poor at establishing and honoring healthy boundaries almost destroyed me. There were two defining moments in my life where I had no choice but to learn to set a boundary.

"The next time I'll be cleaning up your dead body." These words are emblazoned on my memory of the night I was attacked many years ago. The first words I remember after fully regaining consciousness and memory. The officer proceeded to tell me that the second call for domestic violence is typically the last. I don't have full recollection of that night, but I do know that I had to do something. After all, I had a daughter who needed me. Of course, I filed for a divorce and moved hundreds of miles away.

That day, I learned to set a hard boundary. Violence is NOT okay. "Over my dead body" became my phrase for anything that I perceived would harm my daughter or myself. This was the first step in setting boundaries....

But it ultimately was not enough to set boundaries only as they pertain to people I love....

While I could set boundaries in protection of those I love, I used to absolutely stink at setting boundaries with regards to myself and my happiness. I felt guilty or selfish if I considered myself in this regard.

The second defining moment which caused me to take pause and establish boundaries happened much more recently.

A few years ago, from the outside looking in, I was the picture of success. I had a successful career in the male-dominated field of sports medicine. I loved my job, I got to work with elite athletes for a living. I had a beautiful home, an amazing husband, a wonderful family. I had a vibrant social life.

All in all, I was living a great life. Everyone looked at me and said, "You are my life goals! I want to have what you have!" They didn't know me.

They saw the success, they saw the financial security, they saw the career, the house, the family, but what they didn't see was that I was dying on the inside. There were days that I would go into my closet and just cry. I would come home from work two hours past my shift, completely depleted with no time or energy for my husband, my family, to take care of myself, and I was in physical pain for years toward the end of my career in sports medicine.

I wasn't taking the time to get a massage. When I had an injury, I wasn't letting my body heal. In fact, I did everything I could to get back to work ASAP (to be there for everyone else and not let my coworkers or patients down). I wasn't taking care of myself, and I should have known better because I was in sports medicine. It was everything that I preached, nothing that I practiced.

I was spending so much of my day pouring out to everyone else at work, putting on the happy face there... to the point of burnout... and not feeding the needs of my family or myself at home due to my exhaustion. I would complain and "vent" constantly at home about the demands of my job, but then I would turn around and go back... again and again and again.

It was so bad that I had actually tried to quit my job... 3 times over the course of 2 years. Each time I allowed the director to talk me into staying, just cutting my official hours...and I would give in thinking about how busy the program was, what would happen to my coworkers, they were overwhelmed as it was... and who would take care of my clients?

I didn't realize how bad I had gotten until my husband and I went on our anniversary vacation to a private island intending to spend quality time together. It was supposed to be perfect. Guess what happened the first night? We had a World War 3 screaming and crying match in public at the restaurant. It happened because he wasn't getting the quality time that he needed from me. He asked if it was time to consider a divorce.

GUT PUNCH. I was in shock. I had no idea that my burnout, my depletion, and my lack of boundaries could cost me my happiness. I said to myself, "Holy crap! What am I going to do? This is the man of my dreams, I love him so much, I want to spend my life with him! He isn't getting what he needs from me, I'm not giving it to him because I don't have anything left."

I had spent the last 19 years giving my career EVERYTHING, but it wasn't giving back. I had lived a life for my J.O.B. and to raise my daughter… I kept saying, "when she is grown, then I will shift out of hyperdrive" or "when I have enough money in the bank, I'll work normal hours"… who was I kidding?

I was about to lose everything I had worked so hard to achieve… because I hadn't set any boundaries. While my family was the top priority in my life, I had allowed a job to overstretch into my family time… even if I wasn't "on the clock" I was thinking about work or trying to get ahead on a program or planning out how to better manage my caseload (which I took on to not overburden or to lighten the load of others)

I had to find a way to change this. The very first thing I did was get a coach. We're all blind to ourselves. We all have blind spots, and that's exactly why I am such a firm believer in coaching and having someone there that can see in those spots that we just can't.

I was absolutely blind in the fact that I was giving everything I could in my career, and everything that meant success to everyone else, but I didn't see what was right there, and most important. It made me realize that I had to reassess what my priorities were, and together with my coach, I was able to set boundaries in my life. This was so pivotal for me, I decided to become a coach and make this my life's work.

I want to show you how to do the same so that you don't have to get to that World War 3 breaking point before you begin living a healthy and happy life filled with joy and self-care.

" Your capacity to say no determines
your capacity to say yes to greater
things"
~ E Stanley Jones

Exercising Our No

What boundaries do we need to set? How do we show up? How can we continue to set these boundaries for ourselves and honor what we need so that we can show up even better in every aspect of life because now our cup is full? There's an art to boundary setting, it's the art of saying, "No."

When we first start exercising our NO, it may look quite different than what we would hope to show to the world.

For example (and I don't recommend this approach, but if it's your best first step feel free to use it), as I was learning to exercise my NO, it happened that my husband was being promoted to associate in his firm. As part of this promotion, we traveled to the corporate headquarters for a special dinner honoring the new associates... This was about 2 months after our world war 3 almost divorce situation, and full disclosure: we were BOTH attempting healthy boundaries.

Here we are, at this special dinner, and an executive approaches us (and a few others) and begins to talk...about the expectations of associates: the company takes care of their associates, yada yada, because the associates put the company and work over EVERYTHING else... family, spouses, vacations.... you get the idea... WAIT, WHAT???!!!

I was sitting there, trying to put that filter on and set a healthy boundary from a place of love... when "OVER MY DEAD BODY" very emphatically escapes my lips. I might have even shouted it....

GASP. Oh $hi@!!! What did I just do? It just slipped out... I couldn't help it. And now the exec is looking at me...

along with everyone else in earshot... and my husband is too... not in the "oh baby, thanks for sticking up for me" sort of way BUT in the "I CAN'T BELIEVE YOU SAID THAT! I MIGHT LOSE MY JOB! And we are leaving right now before I blow a gasket!" sort of way.

So you can see, boundaries can be a challenge (especially at first)... if I had spoken up a bit sooner, perhaps at the beginning of the conversation (where things were not in alignment with our decision to put our relationship first and work on quality time). If I had perhaps walked away...ALL THE WHAT IF's went through my head...

Had an effective boundary been established initially, it might not have gotten to that blow my stack point.

The reality is that boundaries were difficult for me. They continue to be a challenge. I've included the tools in this book I have learned. I am using the boundaries I have managed to set, and honor... The truth is, I'm not sure where I would be without them. I am excited to share them with you!

Are you ready to establish and maintain healthy boundaries in your life?

Reading a book is great, but if you are like me, you've read books before with the best intentions of making it happen, putting the gems into action ... and ultimately never following through.

Let's change that. At each step of this book, I will have an action step for you to implement strategies for setting and honoring healthy boundaries. Beginning now.

Action Steps:

If you are truly ready to take action, let's make it real.

- Email me with the subject line "I'm ready for life with boundaries"
- jengaudet@jengaudetcoaching.com
- In the subject line put "I'm all in"
- In the email put "I'm all in" with the boundaries you want to set and hold.

I'm happy to offer this container for accountability for you as you set your intention.

Permission Slips-How We Allow People To Speak To Us

When we think about permission slips in this context, consider what it was like when you were a kid, when you had to get a hall pass to go to the bathroom in school. That hall pass was PERMISSION for you to be in the hall so that you could use the restroom.

If a teacher caught you in the hall without that hall pass, it spelled trouble...

We give people permission slips for various things as we let them into our lives. For example, I give you permission to be friends with me you give me permission to be friends with you.

When we cross the boundary, and we say something that's not OK, for example, it is not OK for someone to make a sexual remark to me in a professional setting. I don't care what gender you are, you may not do that. I'm not giving you permission to do that, I visualize taking that permission slip away, establishing that firm boundary, being crystal clear in my communication of what is acceptable and what is not.

As a society, we have become so politically correct and so worried about hurting the other person's feelings if we speak up for ourselves. Essentially, we've given them permission to say whatever they want to us or to treat us in whatever way. That's just not OK. We need to stop that. We need to take that permission slip back and say no, you no longer have permission to demean me. You do not have permission to make me feel bad about myself.

A permission slip is something that you can visualize in your mind when you have not set boundaries, but you want to start setting boundaries. Another example: OK, you've given that person permission to comment about your weight for the last 10 years, and that's how they know you. That's how they've been accustomed to you. It's OK with them because you haven't set the boundary. But today you decide that is a boundary and it's not OK anymore. You can visualize, "I am taking the permission slip away from you to make any comments about my weight, or my outward appearance." Having that visualization is really powerful for us as we learn boundaries. Now you can think, "I am taking the permission slip away;. You don't have permission to talk about my weight in a demeaning manner anymore." It helps us to communicate effectively and honor where we are now. We are no longer that person who allows others to shame us... it also means when they make "shaming" comments, we no longer allow those comments to mean anything about us... We do not allow their words to impact us negatively.

I have been in the boardroom giving a presentation, as a woman that means that I am wearing a professional length skirt, and after I am done had one attendee comment on my legs. Not okay with me! My response? "You don't have my permission to comment on what my legs look like. It's inappropriate and unwelcome, especially in this setting." Set the clear expectation and boundary.

This hasn't been an isolated incident. I've given a presentation as a business owner on a large stage, and people have come up in the back of the room afterward and commented on my appearance. No, you don't have permission to say I like your legs. I mean that is just not OK! You do not have permission to say that to me, it's disrespectful. In my mind, I am like no sorry there is the boundary. We let someone else know clearly you don't have permission and I'm not giving it to you I am not giving you a permission slip to do or say that.

One of my clients attended my boundaries workshop (the basis for this book). She was in a relationship where they both are income earners, and they both are partners, but she allowed him to make her feel unworthy. He would make backhanded comments about her size and tell her she was overweight. Maybe she was 10 pounds overweight by society standards, but she allowed him to take away her self-confidence over time. It was so much more than just about the weight, even while she was on a weight loss journey through lifestyle habit change. She had given him her permission to speak to her like this. In the workshop, we talked about the permission slip and how we own our own power. We talked about things like you really can't make me feel bad about myself unless I give you permission to do that. What was happening was she was giving him permission to belittle her. She needed a boundary. "I do not give you permission to speak to me in that way I have too much respect for myself and too much respect for you to allow you to demean me or to belittle me." That was what she took away from the workshop. She used what she had learned. This led to a big fight with tears, screaming, the whole nine yards. After that, she hired me as her coach. As we started working together, she said, "You know this is really hard." My reply was that the 1st time that we set a boundary like this on someone who's been demeaning us, it is hard. Reclaiming our power, setting boundaries is a PROCESS. It doesn't happen overnight. However, with 1% improvement each day, practicing our boundaries will eventually simply become a part of who we are, will become much easier.

The moment we stop giving another person permission or power over us is the moment we stop reacting to what they say. They are saying things to get an emotional reaction out of us. When we say, "I don't give you permission to say that to me any way anymore you may not speak to me in that manner it's disrespectful" the initial response is often anger. But the next time they say something like that from a place of love we can say, "I do not give you permission to speak to me that way I have too much respect for myself and too much respect for you." As you do that over time, they see you're not giving them permission to trigger you anymore. You do not have an emotional response, and over time, they stop, and they start to honor what you're saying. You don't have permission to comment on my weight. You don't have permission to comment on my lifestyle choices. I love you. I respect you, but you do not have permission to disrespect me. I respect your choices, you respect mine. It's just a manner of setting your boundaries from that place of respect. Respect for yourself and respect for them.

Maybe your family member has a different religious belief, and they're very interested in converting you. You say, "Aunt Susie, I respect you for your religious beliefs. I will never be derogatory of what you believe I would really appreciate it if you respected my beliefs." It's the art of respectfully disagreeing. But setting that boundary and not giving people permission is such an important skill to learn.

Action Steps:

- Grab a journal (or send me another email)
- Answer this question: Where have you given permission slips in your life that are just NOT OK with you?
- What permission slips are you ready to revoke?

Completely Worn?

How do we know it's time to set a boundary?

Are you sick and tired of being sick and tired?

Maybe you're in a job that you find yourself not able to be excited about?

Are you experiencing low energy?

Maybe you've lost all will to do anything aside from vegging in front of the TV?

Perhaps, you physically make yourself ill because you don't make use of your vacation time and become completely overwhelmed and depleted.

Where has all the time gone, right?

Listen, it's the human experience to wear more than one hat in a day. You're not just an employee. You're an employee, a parent, a partner, or spouse. You handle the household, and you're also the gardener, the carpenter, the plumber, the candle-stick maker. You wear multiple hats, and that uses up your time. If you're not separating all of the hats you wear, you can't take the time to refill your cup. This is where boundaries come into play.

Let's talk about what stops us from setting boundaries. Think about the last week. In the last week, what is it you wish you really had time for? Even if you didn't have the resources for it, just think about what you wish you had time for last week. I'll use family obligations as an example. Work is a part of life, but work is something that you can easily set boundaries around. Family obligations are another part of life and something that can be a bit trickier because there are a lot of emotions tied to them. If you're not setting a firm boundary on your work obligations, like leaving work on time, then you're letting your work spill over into your personal time. Your battery between work and personal life is being drained. You're not honoring your personal obligations by letting your work obligations bleed over.

Action Steps:

- Plan a firm stopping time for work or whatever activity is unbalancing your life.
- Plan this for one day this week or next and note in your journal what opened up for you afterward.

"Saying no can be the ultimate self-care"

~ Claudia Black

Understanding Our Priorities

In order to completely understand what is important and how to establish those effective boundaries, we must first understand what our priorities are in life. There are no wrong answers here. At different stages in life, you may notice you have different priorities… and that is perfectly okay and even normal.

I would like to invite you to take a moment RIGHT NOW. Don't put this off until later, feel free to make use of the worksheet or grab a journal.

What are YOUR top 5 priorities in life?

Some common priorities include a higher power, giving back, spouse/partner, children, parents, health, financial security, a place to live, career or business, friends, social life...

There truly are no wrong answers, and there is no room for judgment. Whatever YOUR priorities are, they are perfectly RIGHT for YOU right now in your life. It is also ok if you revisit this exercise next year and those have changed. In fact, I recommend to all of my clients to

reassess their top 5 on a quarterly
basis.

Action Steps:

Write Down Your Top 5 Priorities

1.__________________________________

2.__________________________________

3.__________________________________

4.__________________________________

5.__________________________________

" Sometimes, we need to say no so that
we have more time to say yes"

~ Suzette Hinton

Honoring Your "Yes" & Your "No" - in your Life

List your TOP 5 Priorities in Life:

1._________________________________

2._________________________________

3._________________________________

4._________________________________

5._________________________________

GREAT!!! Now that You've discovered your top 5 priorities in life, I would like to CHALLENGE you to take an objective and hard look at your life and calendar.

Many times we wonder why we lack the time for what's most important to us... we put off playing with our kids because we don't have time or the house needs to be cleaned... and all of a sudden, our kids have moved out of the house (which still isn't perfectly kept), and we are still grinding away wondering where the time went.

Let's DISRUPT that pattern TODAY!!!

Get out your calendar/ task list/ however you plan your week.
Review the next 7 days on your calendar. Feel free to use the handout to complete this exercise.

Look at EVERY event, appointment, task scheduled for the next 7 days. I would like to invite you to consider each one of these to-dos on your list and compare them to your top 5 priorities.

Write which priority (if any) of the 5 corresponds to each event.
Make a list of all activities which are in alignment with your top 5 priorities, and a separate list of all activities which are NOT in alignment with your current top 5 priorities.

The challenge is to cancel ONE of the activities NOT in alignment with your top 5 priorities in life TODAY. In the next 24 hours.

OPEN up that time for yourself so that you can honor what is most important to YOU!!!

If you're like me, and you are justifying how every single appointment and task on your list is in alignment…. I am going to call BS on you right now. Because I too am a master at justification… and it takes one to know one!!

Part of this process is taking all emotion out of your decisions… if there is a convoluted explanation why something aligns with your priorities, NEWSFLASH: it really doesn't.

If you are truly having a difficult time with this exercise, I would like to invite you to ask a few other questions through the process:

1. Am I inspired/ excited about this task/appointment/to-do item?

2. Do I FEEL obligated to follow through with this task/appointment/to-do item?

Many times, feelings and emotions are excellent indicators of alignment with our values. For example, feelings of obligation or guilt if I cancel this event I REALLY don't want to attend...or shame over "why DON'T I want to do this" or "shouldn't I desire to do this?" generally are fantastic clues that these are events/tasks/appointments out of alignment.

Have you ever agreed to do something in the moment and then gotten home and wondered why the heck you said yes in the first place? You either don't have the time or desire to do it! By saying yes in that moment (without stopping to feel into it) you've said no to your top 5 priorities.

Healthy boundaries are about shifting that in the other direction! Saying NO to those things that don't inspire you, so you open up space to say YES to your top priorities, to that which inspires and energizes you!

Action Steps:

- If you haven't determined your top 5 priorities, do it RIGHT NOW.
- Don't wait! Put down the book and grab your journal.

The next part of the book only works if you know what is important to you!

Review the next 7 days on your calendar.

List all activities in your calendar that support your top 5 priorities in life:

1.________________________________

2.________________________________

3.________________________________

4.________________________________

5.________________________________

(continue as long as it takes as you eye your work and personal calendars)

List all activities in your calendar that do NOT support your top 5 priorities in life:

1._______________________________

2._______________________________

3._______________________________

4._______________________________

5._______________________________

(continue as long as it takes as you eye your work and personal calendars)

Choose and circle at least ONE activity that does NOT support your top 5 priorities that you will cancel in the next 24 hours.

Make a commitment to yourself to cancel that activity by WRITING it down. Here, or in a journal. Sign it. Tell someone else for accountability. DO IT.

As I mentioned before, just reading this is great, but if you don't actually TAKE ACTION, what is the purpose? Let's start honoring priorities and setting boundaries RIGHT NOW.

The rest of the book will be here when you are done, I promise!

Once you've reviewed your calendar and decided to cancel something that doesn't support your top 5 priorities, the next step is to recognize that this is a process.

After all, If setting and honoring healthy boundaries were easy or natural, you'd already been doing it!

In order to set ourselves for inevitable success, it's time to brainstorm what might interfere with you actually canceling that event from your calendar, and prevent something else that is outside of your top 5 to make its way into that newly freed space/time.

Ask yourself, "What might get in the way of following through with this challenge?

YES! I am asking you to brainstorm your excuses…

Let's get real, we all self-sabotage. We all have stories we've been conditioned to believe about ourselves. They may sound something like: if I take this time for myself, someone else might suffer. If I spend this money on myself, someone else might not have enough. If I succeed at this job, someone else might feel less than confident moving forward… They may sound like AFTER I do all these things THEN I will deserve to take a break….

Whatever your stories are, this is the time to get raw and real. We ALL have them. It's part of the behavioral conditioning of our society. The good news is if we were conditioned into them, we can be conditioned OUT of them… and this is a great way to start.

Take a moment and brainstorm everything that might get in the way… and the solutions to each obstacle. This is called setting yourself up for inevitable success. I recommend finding an accountability partner, a loved one or a friend, and sharing your actions with them asking for their support and to hold you accountable.

Feel free to use the handout in the appendix or a journal... but whatever you do, don't skip this step.

Yes, it's uncomfortable. Yes, change is challenging... but it's only uncomfortable until it becomes comfortable. This is the first step to choosing to say YES to living your life, to becoming fully alive, and living life on purpose.

Let's get back to our lesson in boundaries.

Was work your number 1 priority?
Did it even make the list?

If you're working overtime and you're too tired for the top five things on your list, how are you showing up in your life? Are you showing up as your best self? So what happens when you're not showing up as your best self? You get tired, you feel frustrated, stressed, maybe some guilt or disappointment? Either way, what you're feeling because of this bleeding over, is exactly what your loved ones and your top 5 priorities are feeling too.

The names have been changed in the upcoming stories to protect privacy.

CLIENT STORY #1 Life without Boundaries: Healthcare provider, Michael, working 60-80 hours per week in busy private practice, taking care of patients and employees... exhausted all day long, frustrated that he never seemed to have energy or time for his family, wife/kids, social life or to even get to the gym. He was carrying a bit of extra weight, sluggish, and even got to the point where he didn't want to get out of bed in the morning. He questioned if he even wanted to remain a physician. His health, his relationships, his fulfillment in life were suffering. But he had employees to pay, patients to treat, mouths to feed.

Journey to boundaries: All his life he believed it was SELFISH to take time for what he enjoyed. He believed that somehow it would take time away from his wife and kids. He believed that if he stuck to an 8-5 he wouldn't be able to help enough people. He believed that he had to give until it HURT. After attending my boundary workshop, he sat down and followed the action steps: listing top priorities, looking at his calendar, limiting 1 appointment slot each week until he had managed his time back to an 8 hour day rather than the 10-12 hour clinic days he was carrying. He hired me as his personal coach to take it up a notch and work on the mindsets and limiting beliefs which kept pulling him back towards over-delivering and putting himself on the backburner. He began to schedule a non-negotiable appointment to exercise daily and carved out his morning routine. He streamlined his clinical practices and hired an associate.

Results: He works a 40 hour week, has improved patient outcomes and patient satisfaction, he enjoys his life again, having time to play with his kids and QT with his wife. You know you've made progress when your client's wife sends you a lovely thank you note that says "Thank you for bringing my husband back." That spoke volumes. Through coaching, he was able to set and maintain healthy boundaries, grow his practice, AND reclaim his life. By setting boundaries, by honoring his self-care, by setting non-negotiable appointments for his PRIORITIES in life, He now has a growing practice, serves more patients, has improved outcomes, has time to give back in his community, and has quality time with his family. Learning to say NO re-energized his body, reignited his passion for medicine, allowed him to reconnect to his purpose, and allowed him to once again LIVE his life.

The same approach bleeds the other way. Not prioritizing your work at all can lead to you not doing your best work, and can cause issues there as well. In this case, with this exercise, it gives you an opportunity to think. You need to consider what your priorities are and how to manage them in order to give the right amount of energy to the needs that have to be met by yourself and your loved ones and work. How can you move forward in a way that doesn't allow for this bleeding over to happen? Ask yourself. If it's six o'clock and you said "Come hell or high water, at six o'clock I'm walking out the door because this is my boundary in place to protect my valuable personal priorities" what would happen? Would the work still be there tomorrow? What would that open up for you?

Client # 2: Paula's LIFE WITH NO BOUNDARIES
50-60 hour workweek, checking emails before getting to work at home, answering work phone calls after getting off work, checking emails, and meeting during my nonexistent lunch hour. Very limited personal time to spend with my son, family, and friends. Trying to finish up all of my personal things on Saturday

and Sunday. Being on call and not being able to be fully present in any part of my life. Fatigue, Burnout, Excessive Weight Gain, Skin Breakout, Stress Reaction, Sleepless Nights.

Paula's JOURNEY TO BOUNDARIES

As I started my journey to installing boundaries, I realized my entire adult life, I had NO boundaries

During many coaching sessions, I had to explore why I did not implement boundaries, and I discovered that I was not choosing me or the people or things that I said were important to me.

I was choosing, work, money, and a mindset that I did not deserve to have a choice in where I wanted to allocate my energy

Week after Week. Tear after Tear. After answering the many difficult questions, the Boundaries began to become consistent in my life.

Each week I challenged and pushed myself outside of my comfort zone to set a boundary with work and my life.

As time passed, I showed myself that I could live my best life with boundaries.

Each boundary provided balance and redefined and reshaped my entire life and mindset

With the guidance of my coach and intentional action steps, my new story is

....

Paula's LIFE BOOMING WITH BOUNDARIES

40-45 hour workweek, turning my work phone off when I get home, Uninterrupted family dinners, healthy eating by taking time to cook and meal prep, working out 3-5 times a week, practicing yoga and meditation to reduce my stress. I am sleeping 6-8 hours a night and waking up refreshed.

TODAY, I am healthy, energetic, and productive. All because I set boundaries for work and my life with the assistance of my coach.

Boundaries are giving yourself permission to honor yourself and those things that are most important to you, like quality time with your spouse. If you're working extra hours and ignoring your priorities, who are you giving your power away to? What permission are you granting to someone else for your valuable time?

You deserve the right to honor your priorities in your life.

Read that again.

YOU deserve the RIGHT to HONOR YOUR priorities in YOUR life.

Honoring your boundaries is the only way that you can show up in the way that you're meant to show up in this world. You should be making a difference in your life and the lives of those around you, and you can't do that if you're busy being tired and resentful.

Thinking a little differently about overtime now?

So, let's storm this barricade! Where in your life are you saying yes, when you really mean no? When are you saying, "Sure" when you really want to say, "I don't want to do that" or "I have other obligations." By setting boundaries, you're saying yes to your health, family time, and to the opportunity to fill your cup and only say yes when you are inspired to, not because you feel obligated to.

What might happen if you live your life in a way that honored your boundaries? How would your life be impacted? How would it impact your friends? How would you feel if you were honoring your boundaries and doing what was most important to you? What emotions come up? How would you feel about that?

You'd feel recharged, right? You'd feel fulfilled? A sense of freedom? If you're honoring your boundaries and you're feeling free and fulfilled, then your cup is full. When your cup is full, how do you show up at work the next day? Refreshed? Ready to take on your tasks? Positive and productive? Yes! Let's do a little activity.

Healthy Boundaries: Honoring Your YES by Learning to Say NO

Where are you saying YES in life when you actually want to say NO? Where in life are you feeling UNINSPIRED/OBLIGATED?

What emotions drive you to say YES to events/opportunities you do not wish to be a part? What emotions build up when you consistently say "YES" in these situations?

What positive intention or purpose do these emotions serve?

Where in life would you like to be saying YES but aren't currently? What INSPIRES YOU?

What is getting in your way? Why don't you experience this NOW?

What might you need to let go in order to honor your YES, your priorities? (See handout in appendix)

What if by saying NO you are actually saying YES to something more important to you?

What are you opening up, where are you able to show up fully 100% present as your best self by saying YES to what INSPIRES you?

We know that boundaries are the ultimate form of self-care and self-love. Don't confuse this for being selfish. The story most of us have heard our whole lives is that we can't devote so much to ourselves because it's selfish. It's selfish for you to not take care of yourself because then you're showing up resentful, tired, full of stress and anxiety. Are you really spreading the love in all of that? No, you're not. If you're practicing self-care, and you're happy and healthy, recharged, fulfilled and feeling good, are you spreading the love? Yes, you are. See the distinction?

In the space below, I'd like you to jot down a few things that you know traditionally you're obligated to do certain things, and when you show up, you know you don't really want to be there.

What feelings come up when you are made to say yes to these things?

Now tell me, how can you change each one of those things? How can you turn it around?

Maybe you're telling your friend that you can't help them move because you've got plans already with your husband. Maybe you're obligated to self-care, and you can't make it to an event that your friend is putting on. Saying yes every time doesn't make you a hero, it makes you reject your priorities and reject yourself. Of course, the "no" is coming from a place of love, but it isn't a bad thing to say no. You are honoring your boundaries. You can always decline with love and suggest another day or time that would work for you better, but the first priority is you and your boundaries.

Action Steps"

- Don't move ahead until you have completed the above section

Why Don't We?

THE LIES WE TELL OURSELVES:

- I Don't have TIME (take me for

Example: I suffered a pretty bad sinus infection when I was in medical school. I didn't want to make an appointment and decided it would sort itself out, convinced I didn't have time to make an appointment for the doctor for myself because I can't take time away from my clinical rotations, it will put my coworkers in a bind and who will see my patients? Also, how would it impact my clinical rotation scores? I can't take time away from my daughter, because I already work 5 days a week in the clinic and have limited time already. What if I miss out on something important for her? The reality, by putting off that appointment to the doctor to care for myself, I ended up with a pretty heinous ear infection and vertigo which prevented me from being able to stand or walk without holding onto the wall. I needed a few days off (instead of a couple of hours) and required more assistance caring for my daughter (who was a toddler at the time). I also showed up less than 100% for a couple of weeks.... plowing through my work and personal responsibilities.

The reality: WE all have enough time for what is most important, we simply don't honor our priorities and set the boundaries, in this case, my health.)

- I CAN'T spend the MONEY

(Let's explore one of my client's who believed this to be truth. Meet Sharon, an attorney who owns her own law practice but struggled with boundaries.

Life before boundaries: She worked all hours of the day (literally working until midnight or 2 am most days and beginning again at 7 am the next day) and was completely exhausted, depleted. Her business was growing rapidly, and she was tending to her clients, her employees, her business, but her personal life was falling apart. Her marriage was rocky at best, she had no social life to speak of because her business and her work consumed her life. She believed if she stepped away, it would all fall apart. The problem was she knew she needed help but didn't want to spend the money on herself to get that help. She believed if she spent the money on a coach to help her establish boundaries, it would negatively impact her business and her personal life. What if the kids needed that money for sports? What if her husband needed that money for something else. She believed it was selfish to spend money on herself and shamed herself for being unable to set and honor a healthy schedule and boundaries on her own. Why should she spend money on something she should already know how to do... Ultimately, she had a breakdown. Her spouse was discussing separation, and her business seemed to be running faster than she could keep up.

The intervention: She hired me as her coach and began to establish non-negotiable family time. Through the step by step process outlined in this book plus mindset work, she learned the art of saying NO. She learned the art of setting and maintaining healthy boundaries.

Life with boundaries: Sharon has stopped bringing work home, with a hard stop at 7 pm and experiences quality sleep again. Her energy is restored, and her business continues to grow profitably. She has found more opportunities to delegate at work. She has found time to actually attend her children's sports events. In fact, she has hired another paralegal and another assistant to offload her time so she could do what her business needed her to do: serve her clients and run the business. More importantly, she continues to spend money on her self-care, because she realized how important it is that she is showing up her best self: properly nourished, energetic, rested, and fully present, which requires regular workouts, coaching, a housekeeper once per week, …Sharon now believes she deserves to take the time she needs for herself. She believes she deserves to spend the money to care for herself so that she can show up powerfully in the world, serving her clients, and caring for her family. She is not only living, she is THRIVING.

- I don't DESERVE to honor my priorities…Sometimes,   our belief structures cause us to believe that anytime we honor what is important to us we are taking away from others, that we do not deserve to have our wants met, that we should be happy with our lot in life. Sometimes, this can be exacerbated when we are the ones standing on the pulpit preaching that self-care is selfish, that money is the root of all evil, that we should trust and place all aspects of our life in the hands of a higher power.

This client, we will call Sam, was a preacher who also owns a business, is a husband and father.

Life before boundaries: He gives until it hurts, often taking care of those he serves before paying his own bills, and lives a life of struggle. Life without boundaries in his life looks like this: He works 10-14 hour days Monday through Saturday. He preaches Saturday night and Sunday. He leads Bible studies on Tuesdays and Wednesdays. While all of that is going on, his home is in duress, needing TLC desperately. His business is barely making ends meet, as he frequently takes time away to tend to "emergencies" of his church community. This results in putting his livelihood on the backburner. He hasn't had a day off (unless he has been severely ill) in years, so many years that he could not recall the last time he actually had a day off where he did something he enjoyed. When asked what brings him joy, he couldn't find anything that didn't involve taking care of someone else's needs, as he identified completely with his role. As a result, he was losing himself in the process.

Intervention: Sam attended the boundaries workshop upon which this book is based. He took to heart many of the ideas presented and worked through the process above and also learning to say No. He realized he needed additional support, and was challenged by his limiting beliefs and mindset. He reached out for individual coaching.

Together we began to slowly set boundaries, starting with an hour less of work per day, adding in non-negotiable time with his wife, and even prayer time for his morning routine.

Life with boundaries: Sam now works 7-4 with a solid lunch break Monday - Friday. He has hired two employees to help him with his business. He works 4 hours on Saturdays currently. He is home in time for family dinner with his wife and family daily. His business is not only making ends meet, but he is almost to the point where he can step away from the day to day and truly work on the business instead of in the business, freeing more time. As a result of setting his own boundaries, he is now implementing them with the members of his church community, honoring his pastoral duties in set times while teaching them about boundaries through his example. He feels energized, no longer worries about money, and has reclaimed joy in his life. He has discovered that he enjoys writing and teaching and has begun writing his first book to honor his creativity. In his growth, with the joy he now experiences, those around him have noticed the difference, and as a result, his relationships have improved.)

- If I take time/money for myself, someone else won't have enough

- It's selfish to take care of myself

THE EMOTIONS AROUND these Lies:

- GUILT

- FEAR of REJECTION/standing out/not being good enough/what others might think

- Resentment

- SHAME

THE OLD BELIEFS:

- The other person getting what they want/need is more

Important than me getting what I want/need

- I am not special/significant enough...
- I am not GOOD enough as I am...

Many of my clients have shared this story. Let me know if this sounds familiar: I will honor my self-care WHEN I have x dollars in the bank... when I have achieved my next certification... Pretty much anytime we put qualifications on our priorities, it falls into this category. Many times, the non-income-earning spouse shares this story. For example, a client of mine, Sarah, took a sabbatical for health reasons from her job as a nurse.

Life before boundaries: After many years of caring for everyone but herself (her patients, her children, her spouse, her community), she found herself overweight, with Type II diabetes, high blood pressure, and physically unable to do many of the activities she enjoyed with her husband and children: hiking, biking, kayaking, even bowling. As a result, and coming from the medical world, she chose to have weight loss surgery, but even though the weight was coming off and her physical health was improving. As a result, she carried shame. Why did she need a procedure to assist with weight loss? Why had she let her health get out of hand? Sarah listened to those around her, those on social media, and the people in her community ask these questions. She allowed these questions to mean she wasn't good enough to do it on her own. She allowed it to mean she was weak... As a result, she felt she couldn't handle the journey. She felt that she didn't deserve to join a gym, that she didn't deserve to spend money as she's already spent so much on a procedure and was not currently earning an income.

Intervention: We began coaching, discovered her priorities, and where in life her priorities were not being met. After she attended one of my boundaries workshops and realized she didn't even know her own priorities. We slowly explored her non-negotiables, those things which helped her show up fully in her life. We discovered she was passionate about giving back but wasn't because it "wasn't her money, she wasn't working for it," She didn't want to spend money on a gym to get her body moving in a way to be able to enjoy life and return to work, because she personally had not earned that money.

Life with boundaries: Sarah was able to return to nursing part-time (their family situation allowed for her to stay at home, but she loved nursing and wanted to return), has lost over 100 lbs and is fit enough to hike, kayak, bowl, and enjoy all the active lifestyle activities her family enjoys. She now donates two days a week to a local charity and serves her community. She takes time for her self care, and most importantly, NO LONGER GIVES ANYONE PERMISSION TO SHAME HER over her journey. She now actively speaks and mentors those going through a similar procedure and health journey, because it was important for her to know she was good enough, sometimes we all need support in our own way, and no one has permission to make her feel less than or guilty over her health journey. She has fallen back in love with herself and her life through boundaries, and she shares that with those around her.

- I don't Deserve self-care or to set boundaries because ... (Many of us have felt guilt or shame over taking time for our self-care.

Whether it is the story that someone else needs that time or money more, whether we believe it is somehow bad or selfish to take care of our bodies and our recharge needs, whatever it is we tell ourselves, the reality is we all DESERVE self-care. We all Deserve to honor our priorities, because by setting boundaries, we are able to show up fully in our gifts and share them with the world. We cannot do that if our health fails, or if we are depleted. If we are exhausted, we physically cannot show up for all the reasons we use to keep from taking care of ourselves. Even worse, when our health fails, we no longer can care for ourselves and require assistance from someone else... an argument in favor of self-care and honoring healthy boundaries is actually selfless)

THE TRUTH:

- Our self-care (especially those of us who are caregivers) is INTEGRAL

- If our cup is empty, we cannot pour out into anyone else

- We are in a state of self neglect....it impacts everyone around us

- If we are feeling guilt or shame, resentment... what are we pouring into our children/spouses/those for whom we are caregiving? Are we showing up as our best selves? What example are we setting?

- If we are tired, depleted, even sick.... How are we showing up? Can we even show up?

- There is always enough TIME and MONEY for those things which are most important... and our health tops that list

The SOLUTION:

- Prioritize: set time aside (no matter how small) for self-care

- List the activities which fill your cup, incorporate 1 per day to recharge yourself

- Plan: budget accordingly to ensure inevitable success with filling your cup

- Learn how to say NO with love, to hold your time for self-care sacred

SELF-CARE MENU:

- Varies for everyone but can look like:
- Nutrient-dense food at mealtimes
- Getting movement minutes in your day
- Dancing like nobody's watching
- Singing your favorite song at the top of your lungs
- Taking a warm bath
- Deep breathing
- A brief walk outside
- Reading a book

- Getting a massage
- Playing with a fur baby
- Taking a nap
- Mani/Pedi (even if you do it yourself!)
- Playing your favorite sport
- Make a list of activities that light your soul up... and choose one for your day!

Before you say, "I don't have time" Here are a bunch of quick 1-5 minute "recharges"

- Breathing: 1 minute of intentional breathing 5-5-5 breath
- 7-minute exercise routine
- 1 minute "mental breaks"

- Step outside and sun gaze or enjoy the sounds/sights
- Find a motivational quote
- Gratitudes
- Face wash

Action Steps:

Replace one old belief with a new belief.

- Write out the old belief in your journal.
- Then, write out your new belief with at least three examples reinforcing that new belief.
- Repeat this activity each day and keep track of how easy it is to find examples which reinforce the new belief.

You can expect your new belief to be about 1% easier to write about each week. Stay persistent.

"Focus is about saying no."

~ Steve Jobs

FEAR

We can definitely feel a bit of fear in the beginning stages of figuring out and then sticking to our boundaries. Have you ever watched a toddler take their first steps? No Fear! How many times does it take a toddler to practice before they perfect walking? It's like a gazillion times, right?   Falling for them is a failure. It doesn't get in their way, they get right back up and try again. Failure doesn't define us. It's what we do with it and how we get back up again.   Listen, the most successful people on the planet fail 80% of the time. You see their successes. You know they're real. Just like a toddler falling on their face, you're going to fall. It might hurt a little, but it's temporary, and you're going to learn to walk eventually. Pretty soon, you'll be running!

Fear is excitement on pause. It's potential energy when it could be used as something constructive for us. Don't be afraid of failure. It's where you learn your biggest lessons. Don't be afraid of falling or being rejected, because when you get back up, and you're accepted, the failure won't mean anything and you'll be living the life you were meant to live.

Actions Steps:

- Go ahead and do that thing you are afraid of failing.
- When you fail, write down what was constructive about the experience in your journal.
- Pay particular attention to what went well, and what learning came from that experience.
- Have FUN with it!

Learning How to Say No from a Place of Love

Saying no is something that people really are challenged with. It is hard to say no. But you can learn how to actually say no from a place of love. Let's look at how we say no to family and the people we love, as well as to how to say no professionally from a place of service. It is a technique.

1st step to learning to say no is learning the art of Pressing Pause.

When someone comes to you and says, "Hey, I want to invite you to come to my ribbon-cutting ceremony, it's tomorrow." The technique is to press pause and say, "Thank you so much for inviting me. I really appreciate the invitation, but I'm going to need to press pause on this and check my schedule." Then I can take the time to look at my schedule and make sure I don't have anything that conflicts. Then I can get back to them. This allows us, instead of just saying no from impulse, to pause, evaluate, and decide.

2nd step is to remove yourself from that situation. A lot of people have a hard time saying no. They don't want to hurt someone's feelings. They say yes out of fear, as a gesture. They don't want to damage the relationship. They don't want the other party to feel rejected. The art is to learn to press pause. Then after you are out of the situation, and that person is no longer in front of you, look at your calendar and decide. Okay, is it something that I feel inspired to do? Rather than when I get there, I'm going to be wishing I were somewhere else or had chosen differently. So after looking at our schedule and deciding, we can call that person back and say, "Hi, I really would love to. Unfortunately, I have a conflict."

Or with a client, if you already have something going on, or you just are not prepared, "Listen, I would really love to work with you right now, unfortunately I couldn't give you 100% of my focus, and I refuse to give you anything less than being 100% present when we work together." That's honoring our integrity. "So let's look at this day and time instead." Then offer an alternative.

With a family member, "Hey, I'm moving. Can you come help us move this weekend?" You can say, "No, have you considered a moving company? Or have you asked ____," and give another option.

Knowing the art of pressing pause is really crucial. Honoring yourself and giving yourself permission to say, "If the answer needs to be given right at this moment, the answer is no, because I can't make an informed decision." You have the right to take the time to evaluate before deciding. Am I emotional? Is it in alignment with my priorities? I don't know if I have that time? Can I manage my energy that day? If an immediate answer is needed, then the answer is always no. Give yourself permission to set a boundary. The boundary to press pause. The boundary to say no if it needs an immediate response. If somebody demands an immediate response, we learn to say, "I would love to be able to say yes. I really appreciate this invitation. Or I completely understand you wanting to know if I can accept you as a client, but I cannot give you that answer at this moment. I need time to make sure that I can at this time."

I personally do this from the space that if I cannot give you 100% of my attention or bring 100% of me to that interaction, then, unfortunately, I can't tell you yes at this moment. The reality is that there are only a few people who will continue to push you for that immediate answer. Many will back off and allow that space for consideration once the boundary is established. This is what happens when you set a boundary. The beauty is that this allows you to take a step back when you are used to saying yes because you feel pressured.

The people that put the pressure on you do it because they are used to getting what they want. Pressuring you (or whomever for that matter) works for them. The basic psychology of selling is to time limit decisions. When we are time-limited, or an immediate response is requested, fear of missing out often causes us to say yes when we really mean no. When you say, "I'm sorry I can't give you that because I can't guarantee I'll show up 100% now," they generally will say, "Well when can you get back to me?" Then you can say, "How about tomorrow." It's really funny because when you set that boundary, a few people get put off and they get angry when you say, "Well then the answer has to be no if it has to be right now." But most people say, "Well, when can you let me know?" That buys you time so you can really come from a place of love and service.

Sometimes you get asked to do something you really don't want to do it. Energetically you don't want that to come across as a rejection. So if you say, "Let me get back to you." It allows you to come back and say it from a different space instead of, "OMG, I don't want to do that."

This is especially important for our children. It helps them learn the skill of delayed gratification. I truly believe that the reason we have such a hard time saying no is that we are in such an instant gratification society. Social media is like yes, yes, yes, yes, yes. You're scrolling through, and you're getting all that stimulus and immediate gratification. But when we tell it our children, even though they might throw a temper tantrum. Let them. They learn the skill set of patience. When we say, "You know why we can't do that right now, let's talk about this later." When we say no, it's important that we show even our young children respect.

So your 2-year-old toddler says, "I want ice cream," Well really what they need is a meal. Delayed gratification can be taught here. We can say, "We're not having ice cream right now, but what we are having is carrots and chicken, so if we're hungry, this is the option." Then when it is time for ice cream, we can show them that learning to delay gratification is a skill set.

Teenagers especially like to have whatever they want RIGHT now. They are also especially susceptible to rejection. So allowing teenagers to see the art of pressing pause really empowers them. In so many areas of life, we have unhealthy relationships. We have peer pressure. When we demonstrate, and we teach through example with our teenagers, they can develop a strong important skill. Learning to say, "That's not what I want to do right now," or, "We're not going to do this right now. Let's press pause and step away." The art of pressing pause and stepping away is powerful. It doesn't even have to be til tomorrow night. Your teenager is presented with something they don't want to deal with they can say, "I'm not entirely sure, let me run to the ladies room, I'll be back," And get away from the situation so that they can clear their mind and decide, is it peer pressure, or do I really want to do it? Is it something that's going to benefit me? Really it's about executive function and learning discernment. I really believe that saying no to our children, saying no to our teenagers, and showing them the art of pressing pause, teaches them to honor and create that boundary.

So if we say "No, we're not going to have ice cream today," then we need to not have ice cream today. Maybe we will have ice cream tomorrow. Or we might schedule when we're going to go for ice cream, but you can't just say yes. It's just setting a boundary and honoring that boundary. We teach that to our children, and then we honor that with our teenagers. It's teaching them critical life skills, so they learn to trust themselves and learn to honor what's important, for that matter what serves them.

Your child comes up with their friend at church and says, "Can Jenny come home with us today, or can I go to Jenny's house?" The best thing to do in that situation is to say, "You know what Susie I will have to think about that, how about you and Jenny go have a conversation right now, and I will discuss this with your father. We'll get back with you." And then when they come back, "You know what, we've already decided that this is not a good day for us, how about if we invite Jenny over next week. Let's talk to Jenny's parents and see if that works for them?"

Say it's Thanksgiving, you're married, your mom wants your time, and maybe your parents are divorced, so your dad wants your time too. Your spouse's family wants your time, and your own family wants your time. Now Mom is pressuring you to dinner, and you say, "You know what Mom, I really would love to come, but unfortunately this year it's time to go see my Husband's side of the family, and so we are not going to be able to attend. Instead, we would love to invite you to a Pre-Thanksgiving get together the night before at our house." Or "let's have something special on Saturday or Sunday so that we can stand that quality time together."

The reason I bring up the holidays is that's the easiest example where everybody tries to cram it all in. We've all had the experience where we try to go to 4 or 5 different gatherings. What happens is you show up, and you're like, "Okay, so I have from 11:00am to 1:00pm here." Then we need to book it across town so we can be there for that. So instead of being present in that moment and joining in on family time, what you're really doing is worrying about your schedule. Instead of enjoying you are thinking about not eating too much, so you have room at the next gathering so that nobody gets offended. And the reality is that when we show up from that space and we're hurrying things. We've ALL been on the other end of that. It is received from a place of, "Oh, they don't really want to be here." It's just a different energy as opposed to saying, "I'm only going to be fully present right here and right now because I'm only going to say yes to one thing that day." Maybe you're there for 3 and a half hours, but you are fully there, and it is truly quality time at the table, gathering, or party. You have the option. You make the choice. It's not a rejection. Instead of saying no its, "I'm not saying no I'm not to be with you on thanksgiving. I'm saying yes I want to be with you on Thanksgiving, but I would love to do it in a way that we have real quality time. In a way that is not rushed. So how about Friday."

Let me give you one more example, and I use this a lot because I personally am married to an introvert. I've got Italian and Cajun roots, so think very big, very loud families. We love to get together. I'm an extreme extrovert, but my husband is an extreme introvert. If he goes to a party, like let's say it's my mom's birthday, and she's having all the family and all the friends, we might decline that invitation because I know that if my husband comes into that scenario, he's going to sit in a corner and be a thundercloud. He's not going to be comfortable, and I'm going to worry about him. So instead of enjoying the event, celebrating and having a real joyous occasion, what ends up happening is we leave early because I've got a bump on the log over in the corner that everybody's asking what's wrong. The only thing that's wrong is he shut down because he's an introvert, he does better with one on one. So when I get that invitation, I respond with, "You know what, I would really love to come, but I would prefer to do something special for you." Or, "Let's go have some real quality time because in a party situation we're going to only get a little bit of time with you when everybody's in competition for time with the birthday girl. So instead let's have an intimate dinner mother, with and father and myself. Somewhere we all can have a meaningful conversation and real quality time."

When you set that boundary, and it's "You know what, I know that you really want quality time with us, and that is the reason for having everyone together, but instead how about we go and celebrate the holiday at another time when we can really spend time with one another." If it's working for you, if you're in an extrovert, by all means, go to the party, say yes to the parties. But if you're an introvert you don't have to miss out, there is no missing out. You can meet with those people individually on your own terms. You can be energetically unchallenged. You're able to conserve your energy and be fully engaged in the interactions you choose.

Now for friends. I have a really close friend with whom I enjoy spending quality time. She and her husband love Country dancing. They love to go drinking and dancing but to country music, and the only kind of music I don't like is country. I love to dance a lot, but I'm not a big line dance person. I'm not really the biggest on socializing over alcohol, because it's not really quality time. So for a long time when we got together as couples, we went country dancing. I can tell you that the challenge was I wasn't honoring that boundary because I wanted to see my friends. So there she is, she's dancing, we're having a good time, but it's loud, it's country music. I'm irritated within 3 songs I'm like, oh I just can't anymore. I'm tense, I can't really hear her anyway because the music is so loud. We start a conversation, and then her husband takes her off to the dance floor to country dance. So the whole night is just this broken communication. What I learned was when she asks me to do that, I go, but with a different set of expectations on myself. I'm not going to go so that I can have quality time with my friends. If I'm going to say yes, I'm going to show up for 30 or 45 minutes just to show up for my friend, and then I'm going to remove myself from that. I'll invite her to the side, and I say, "Hey, I would much prefer we went for a walk and had brunch." I say, "yes, I absolutely want to spend time with you. How about we do it in a way that we don't have to yell to be heard."

So it's the same thing expressing how you are feeling and offering a different solution that meets both of our needs. She is a close friend. She wants the conversation too, it's just it doesn't really work in a situation like this, she's not getting the best of me. The beauty behind it is when that starts happening, it starts being reflected back to me. Now when I invite her to something that she doesn't really feel comfortable about she can say, "I like don't really feel that what if we do something else." It's kind of like this ripple effect. Now when we get together, it's something we both like and we connect on the things we both want to do.

Sometimes, we have a friend who is taking advantage. Rather than enabling them when they say, "Hey Jen. Can you watch my children? I have to work." Something that is happening every weekend, I can say, "Okay, well, let me think about this, I have to get back to you." I press pause and then when I call her back I can say, "I would love to be able to help you, but unfortunately I have plans already. Have you tried your mother? Here is the babysitter that I have been using. Why don't you give her a phone call, she's amazing." Provide another option, but don't give in and give up your boundaries.

How about in business. Angry client calls in while you're with another client. With your clients, you want to be 100% there. The answer is to set boundaries. Turn the phone off. This is very, very hard with computers and texts and emails. All of that is shut down when you're working with someone. This is especially hard for busy caregivers. Establish that boundary in the beginning. It's very important that we are 100% present. I do not accept phone calls, texts, emails, or interruptions while with a client. Let the client know upfront. "There may come a time when we may be interrupted. Just like I won't take a call from you while I'm with another client, I am not going to take a call from them when I am with you." It was very important that I'm all in focused on the person sitting in front of me. When that happens, you've already pre-established it.

You can do this on phone calls too, you can start by saying, "Hi Ms. Jones, I'm so excited to be with you. We have 15 minutes for this call. I just want to reestablish that 2 minutes before the call is going to end, I'm going to interrupt what you are saying and ask if there is anything we need to do in closing before schedule our next call? Because I have to honor my time as I want to be 100% present and honor your time. Then I want to honor the next person's time." In this way, when the time comes you lovingly say, "Ms. Jones do you remember at the beginning of the call when I said that we had 2 minutes left, I would interrupt and make sure that we can come to closure? We have 2 minutes left. Do you feel complete, or is there something else we need to explore? If this is going to take more than 60 seconds, let's go ahead and schedule our next phone call."

It's kind of sandwiched our boundaries and our saying no. We're, in a friendly way, framing the expectations and setting the boundaries. When it's time to transition, we're honoring the boundaries, in a way that we have already predetermined works for them. I generally like to say "Okay Ms. Jones, I'm going to lovingly interrupt you when we have 2 minutes left in the call to honor your time because your time is valuable. How would you like me to do that?" I try to honor what way works for her. I'm asking how do you want to be interrupted, and I'm following suit. Then it becomes more of a professional transition.

In our careers, we always have a choice if we know that this person is not energetically aligned with us, or if we aren't the right fit for his or her needs. Some people are just really not ready. For example, I am a coach: sometimes, I get a call from somebody, and they're really negative. They really want to take a pill to fix them. They don't actually want to do the work. You know that within a couple minutes. First, I set the boundary that I don't offer my coaching services to everybody. It is hard at first when I have to say no to a potential client, especially in a baby business when you need the money. It is 100% of the time always better to say no to that person who is not your ideal client or who is not a match for you. If they come and either they're an energy vampire or if they want a magic pill, they're not ready for coaching. It is my responsibility to say to myself, "Yeah, I need to pay the bills. I really could use it, but no amount of money is worth it." If they're not ready and they're not going to get good results because I can't show up 100%. If they only want a quick fix and they don't want to do the work, in those cases, I know that coaching is not for them. I am out of integrity if I offer them my package. I will still give them value, I'll say, "Why don't you check out this book." Or now I have this book I'll say, "I've got a book." Many times I offer a referral to another service, coach, or practitioner who is a better fit for that person's needs. Whatever it may be, I always give them something of value that they can take the next step.

At the beginning of my coaching practice, I wasn't really good at that. You might laugh at this. At the time, I was charging next to nothing for my coaching services. This person came to me who was completely NOT ready for coaching, they were really looking for a magic wand. I was not comfortable with saying I'm not going to offer my services because I was a baby coach. I was worried about what they would think if I said no. So I said great and asked for a very large amount of money to work with me for 12 sessions, thinking rather than say No and honor my boundaries, I would give them an offer there was no way they would accept. And wouldn't you know they said yes? Every single session sucked the life out of me. They didn't do anything that I asked them to do. For me, coaching is about accountability. Between sessions you're supposed to reach out to me if you get stuck, so we can keep you moving forward. She did none of that. I regretted it every time I showed up. I just absolutely dreaded working with this person. No amount of money is worth that. No amount of money is worth it, because what happens is they don't get a good result, and you don't get a good feeling from it. You start to doubt yourself and whether you can actually do it. No amount of money is worth sacrificing your belief in yourself or your ability to do what you do. You just can't put a monetary value on the impact of something like this. after I took this client, it felt like I made 0 dollars for 3 months because I so hated every session. I couldn't bring 100% of myself because I was out of integrity.

Learning to say no when it's not right for you trusting that you if you only take the right people for you then you know you are in integrity. You know which people who are ready for what you have to offer or are going to do to work. The people that are going to be there for you. When you say no, you're basically saving a space for people who you are meant to work with. I will give that reverse I hired a coach myself for 12 sessions. The 1st 4 sessions were amazing. Then I realized that it was no longer a fit for me. We had a contract. It was non-negotiable for me to pay the contract that I had created with this coach. I walked away from 7 paid sessions. I paid her $12,000 for 12 sessions, so I walked away from $70,000 of my own investment because my time was worth more than what I was getting out of our conversations. So it goes both ways. Fortunately, I haven't entered into another situation like that.

What I tell people is that there's no shame in knowing a client is not the right client. There's no shame in refunding whatever portion of the services you haven't used, or they haven't used and recommending them to someone who has what they need. In fact, to me, that's professional integrity. I learned that one the hard way.

This applies even to people you have never met before. The bell ringers at Christmas. Really anything where you are being asked to give something. I have a client that is very community and civic-minded. He volunteers at his church he is an amazing individual. He asked me this question, "How do I go into the 3rd Ward to minister down there in underserved areas?" See all the people who are asking for money, all the people who are in need and not help. I end up always giving to the point where it hurts. We've all been in this situation. Many of us growing up were taught to give the shirt off our back. We were taught blessed are the poor. We have these faulty money beliefs. So what we do is we give until it hurts. That's what he was doing every single weekend. We discussed knowing that you're going into that situation every week having exactly the number of dollars that you're willing to give away whether it's $1.00 bills $5.00 bills whatever and when you run out, you run out. We set a specific amount of money to give back. When it is gone, it is gone for that time. When that next person approaches you simply say, "I apologize, but I do not have any additional money at this moment."

I always have a sliding scale space for my coaching practice. I only have space for one sliding scale client at a time. I have a waiting list. If you are willing to wait that's great; otherwise I can give you some other options of people who offer sliding scale coaching as well. To the person not able, or willing, to wait, we say no. We can pre-decide what we're willing to give to the bell ringers at Christmas if that's something that you want to do. You know when you're going shopping you are going to see 5 of them. Instead of bringing a $5 bill bring 5 $1 bills. And if that's not a charity that you are giving to this year, then it's perfectly acceptable to say Merry Christmas. It's not a rejection, it's Merry Christmas. I personally don't eat cookies so, but I do like to support the Girl Scouts. What I will do is give whatever amount to the Girl Scouts as monetary donations. You don't have to actually buy the cookies.

The point is you need to have paused before you go out of the house and make the decision about what you are going to do before you go out. I decide if I am willing to help how much am I willing to help, and what is my strategy. That way, as it comes up, you've already got a strategy. You already have a pre-planned way to say, "I wish I could help you, but I can't." A respectful way of saying no.

Now, let's talk about our spouse or partner. People have different hang-ups with their spouse; mine is just saying No from one place of love. OK So let's talk about the obvious one because people like to go to the sexual side of things. And it's a topic that people don't talk about that they need to. You're not in the mood. It's just not working for you right now, and you're afraid that it's going to come off as rejection. This happens for women the most (or at least they talk about it the most), I don't really see it as much for men where they are just sucking it up and doing it anyway (perhaps because they don't want to talk about this). It tends to be the woman for whatever reason. This is a touchy topic. You really don't want to hurt your spouse's feelings, or you don't want him to feel like he's rejected. All of us have been there. I have been there. I've been so exhausted that I'm right now just no. You can talk like that in your head, but the way for it to come out as I really love you, and I really want this closeness, but at this moment in time I do not have the energy. Why don't we schedule a date night? Let's have a date night on Saturday night. That way I can sleep in on Saturday and really be 100% present.

It tends to happen, especially for people who spend all week giving everything we have, everything of ourselves to our clients all day long. Many of us do not set the boundary, then at the end of the day, we're exhausted. We need to learn to manage our energy. We need to learn to say I'm not in that space. It's not going to be enjoyable for me. Because if you're in an intimate relationship, you're exhausted and not fully there you're going to have resentments. Rather than have that resentment, that oh I have to do what's right just suck it up or whatever, giving yourself permission to say, "I really love you can we just cuddle tonight and and have it be alright" will let them know that you still love and care about them that you're not rejecting them.

That's a sticky topic, and it's one that a lot of people struggle with I have experienced where I would prefer it, but my husband has been just tired, and he's like No don't touch me today. That has happened I actually completely respect being in that space. When we start to open that communication, we start to honor that boundary and say, "Not now, but this is not it's not a no it's I don't have the energy or the mental space for this right now can we try again tomorrow." That lets them know that you're not rejecting them. It's such an important communication skill in relationships.

The other big one is with regards to money. One of you wants to buy something, and the other is the money manager. Learning the ability to say, "You know what honey I hear that you really want this, is this an absolute need or is this something that we can plan for? I'm not telling you no I'm just saying how can we make this happen? It's no we're not going to spend $4000.00 on this vacation today let's look at what our options are so we can take a vacation within our budget. Let's plan for it so at it together.

Money and sex are the 2 biggest money issues. We need to learn to effectively communicate with our spouse. Effective communication requires knowing and communicating your boundaries. It's communicating what is it that you're willing to do; what is it that you're not willing to do; and what's in the middle. When you're in a collaborative relationship with someone, and he's a major saver, you tend to be a spender, or however it may look for you. How do we communicate so that I'm making and saving and spending, and he's making and saving and spending, and we both feel good about it? It's a perfect opportunity. When my husband or I need something like a car, we will go shop together, but we will not buy right then on purpose. We try everything on for size. We have conversations about it. We're going to plan for it. When we do buy it one day, we have come to terms with what are we willing to accept and what are we not. We make a plan and put it in place. When a need comes up like I need to brakes on my car well, that is something we have to fix for safety, but we cannot have this negatively impact us. So what are we willing to sacrifice?

If you have the situation where Dad comes home and has all the fun, and mom is the one that has always had to say no, we have to negotiate boundaries. Things like, maybe when you get home you get like. 10 minutes to come in and unwind but then you have to help. We discuss all these kinds of things before they come to a head. It's a matter of awareness so if mom is the disciplinary and a dad is the fun person it's mom's role to step up and say, "OK Dad I'm going to take an hour to myself it is your responsibility now to do these things with the children." That is a very hard thing, especially for women who are stay-at-home mothers. I think in our society we look at the stay at home moms like they don't work. Research not too long ago said that the stay-at-home mom actually has 3 full-time jobs, including taking care of all the kids and oh by the way managing the house and usually the family finances. Often moms feel I don't deserve to take time or money for myself because I am not working a 9-5. Or other peoples needs are always more important. Many women think, "I've been home with the kids all day long, he's been at work, let me just not say anything." That becomes very difficult over time because the reality is she needs to set that boundary. Maybe it is, I'm going to give you 30 minutes to unwind, do whatever you need and relax and then I need for myself or an hour or two as well.

We make a boundary that we're going to share the responsibilities from this moment on. It's just a frank conversation. Things like I'm not going to continue to be the only one who is disciplinary. I expect that when you come home from work, you are going to discipline because that's my downtime. It's a negotiation and communication. You need to learn the ability to say, "I do deserve to take this time for myself." The reality is that if you're going to show up the next day, take care of your children and be a good spouse, you need to step aside and take time for yourself. Otherwise, you're pouring from an empty cup. You become tired and resentful

Action Steps:

1. The next time you have something come up unexpectedly, use the PRESS PAUSE technique and defer the commitment until you know what you can commit.

2. Practice the ALTERNATIVE NO technique by telling a loved one no to their initial ask and offer something else in return.

CONCLUSION:

Here are the most important things to remember in the process of setting boundaries:

1. Write down your priorities. Know your top 5, and stick to them.

2. Schedule non-negotiable appointments. Use these for work-outs, time for your spouse, anything that needs to happen without interruption.

3. Review your calendar, be sure that everything fits your

priorities and that you have your non-negotiables scheduled.

4. Reassess anything that is scheduled that shouldn't be, or that may interfere with higher priority tasks or events or scheduled appointments.

5. Communicate about your boundaries with those around you.

Remember, when you're saying no to something, or canceling an appointment that interferes with something that is priority, (which you can do and not feel guilty about it because it is forming your boundaries) then you are saying yes to something that means more to you. It can be difficult to start, and even to implement, but using communication and repetition until it becomes comfortable and a habit will help. Setting boundaries and living unapologetically as yourself is part of the art of saying no, but it also sets the scene for you to live the life you were destined to live. Don't allow yourself to become resentful, tired, out of time, and bitter. Set healthy boundaries, communicate them effectively, stand by them. Go ahead and draw that line in the sand. It is time in your life to make strong, powerful boundaries that no one is allowed to cross and stand by it. It is time to boldly say about the clear boundaries in your life, "Over My Dead Body!"

CALL TO ACTION:

Fantastic job going through this book and beginning to take action, establishing boundaries and learning the art of Saying NO!

Perhaps, you are ready to dive deeper into healthy boundaries or are ready for additional support learning the art of saying no in your life.

If you've begun taking these steps, and are ready to uplevel your progress.... or you need additional support to simply get started, Go to

- https://jengaudetcoaching.com/boundaries/
- Or send me an email to jengaudet@jengaudetcoaching.com

I look forward to walking beside you for the next step in YOUR process!

APPENDIX:

ACTION STEPS: Really Honoring Your "Yes" & Your "No"

List your TOP 5 Priorities in Life:

1.__________________________________

2.__________________________________

3.__________________________________

4.__________________________________

5.__________________________________

Review the next 7 days on your work and personal calendars.

Make a list of activities scheduled that support your top 5 priorities:

1.________________________________

2.________________________________

3.________________________________

4.________________________________

5.________________________________

Make a list of activities scheduled that do NOT support your top 5 priorities:

1.___________________________________

2.___________________________________

3.___________________________________

4.___________________________________

5.___________________________________

Choose and circle at least ONE activity that does NOT support your top 5 priorities that you will cancel in the next 24 hours.

The activity I will cancel in the next 24 hours is: ___________________

What might get in the way of my
ability to do this?

What are the typical ways I self-
sabotage?

How will I handle the excuses I make
to get out of my own way?

How will I set myself for Inevitable
Success?

Who will I ask to hold me
accountable?

www.ingramcontent.com/pod-product-compliance
Lightning Source LLC
Chambersburg PA
CBHW061755250726
48657CB00001B/128